BURNED Y
BITT

BUT GOD!!! ACTS.

#GODLIAC

God's Genes

Dedicated to All Five of My Children

To my five children, this is for you. You are not defined by what came before you, by what tried to attach itself to the bloodline, or by what the enemy thought he could pass down. You belong to God. His hand is on your lives, His purpose is in your breath, and His identity is greater than anything the world could ever try to name you. You carry God's genes — not by flesh, but by Spirit.

May your lives reflect the fruit of the Spirit, the heart of Christ, and the strength of a new creation. Walk in love, joy, peace, patience, kindness, goodness, faithfulness, gentleness, and self-control. You are chosen, covered, and called. GODLIAC is the one who knows they belong to God, and my children, you are proof that God's fire does not destroy what belongs to Him — it refines it.

What Does "BUT GOD!!! ACTS." Mean?

Throughout this book, you will see this declaration: BUT GOD!!! ACTS. #GODLIAC

This is not just a phrase. It is a divine interruption, a divine appointment, and the evidence of God's presence active and alive in a situation. It is God's authority showing up in power and with demonstration. It is the moment when the I AM THAT I AM steps into the matter Himself, and everything has to respond to His authority.

When God acts, the Red Sea has to part, the walls of Jericho have to fall, and a bush can burn without being consumed. Three Hebrew boys can stand in a fiery furnace and come out without the smell of smoke. Daniel can come out of the lions' den untouched. Jonah can come out of the belly of a great fish with purpose still alive. Dry bones can live again, graves cannot hold what God calls forth, and what is impossible in the natural has to bow to what is possible through Him.

We cannot water God down, put Him in a box, shrink His presence, or minimize His authority. God is love, but He is also holy. He is merciful, but He is also righteous. He is gracious, but He is also a consuming fire. He is not to be handled lightly, explained casually, or reduced to what makes people comfortable. He is God. He is the I AM THAT I AM.

Jeremiah 1:12 declares, "I will hasten my word to perform it." That is God Acts. God watches over His Word to perform it.

Isaiah 55:11 declares, "So shall my word be that goeth forth out of my mouth: it shall not return unto me void..." That is God Acts. God's Word does not leave His mouth empty, return powerless, or fail because the situation looks impossible. When God speaks, His Word carries authority, assignment, fulfillment, and power. When God acts, He is not asking the situation for permission. He is not negotiating with the enemy. He is not waiting for man's approval. He is performing what His Word already declared.

BUT GOD!!! ACTS. means God Himself showed up with His power, His authority, His presence, His Word, and His fire. The act is God moving. The witness is what remains after He moves. The evidence is what His act leaves behind.

That is why I can look at my life and say my scars are a witness, my leg is a witness, my walk is a witness, my survival is a witness, my healing is a witness, my fire is a witness, and GODLIAC is a witness. But the witness only exists because God acted.

So, when you see BUT GOD!!! ACTS. #GODLIAC, read it as the stamp of God's own authority stepping into what man could not fix, what the enemy could not finish, and what the natural could not explain. When God acts, the ending changes, and when God is finished acting, the witness remains.

The Day Water Tried to Put Out the Fire

Before my heart and soul were ever set ablaze for God, my natural body was burned by scalding hot water - the very thing known to put fire out. The enemy came after me with all he had. He was determined to kill me, steal my Ember, and destroy my call.

But the enemy miscalculated. This would come with a price.

I grew up in a small town in Arkansas. We lived in the country, on the outskirts of town, where life was not always easy and everything we had came by faith, effort, and survival. At that time, our hot water heater had gone out, and we could not afford to replace it right away.

My mother was the only parent in the home that day. The only father I knew was away working, so we did what we had to do. We used a large number-three foot tub and heated water on the stove. The water would be carried from the stove to the bathroom, poured into the tub, and then cooled down before anyone got in. That was how we made things work with what we had.

My mother had warned us many times not to run and play while hot water was being carried through the house. She cautioned us that when we saw anyone moving through the house with hot water, we were to move back, stop playing, and stay away until the water had been poured safely into the tub.

Our house had a kind of roundabout layout. You could go from one room into the hallway, and the hallway wrapped around into another room. In that same hallway area, the bathroom and kitchen were connected. So when hot water was carried from the stove to the bathtub, it had to pass through that shared space.

One evening, my siblings and I were running through the house, playing. My mother had already told us several times to stop running and stop playing. My brothers had taken the hot water off the stove to pour it into the bathtub, but my sister realized the stopper was not in the tub. Because my brothers did not want to stand there holding that heavy tub of hot water, they set it down while she went into the bathroom to put the stopper in.

At that very same moment, my brother and I were playing. He was acting like a dog and chasing me. I was backing up, laughing and playing, not realizing the danger behind me. Before anyone could stop me, I flipped backward into the hot water.

My older brother snatched me out immediately, but the damage was already done. The scalding water had burned me so badly that my leg was almost unrecognizable.

My siblings screamed for my mother, who was outside talking to the woodman who had delivered wood for the heater we had in the living room. In the panic of that moment, they wrapped a sheet around me. We did not have a working phone line in the house, and we lived about forty-five minutes from the nearest hospital in any direction. My mother had the choice of taking me to Forrest City, Arkansas, or West Memphis, Arkansas. She chose Forrest City.

By the time we arrived at the hospital in Forrest City, the burns were too severe for them to handle. They had to helicopter me to Memphis, Tennessee, to John Gaston Hospital, which had a burn unit. When they pulled the sheet from my body, parts of my leg were cooked. Other parts were blistered. The skin had come off the whole side of my leg and from my buttocks all the way down my leg. Everything was burned beyond what they believed they could handle.

I was only three years old when scalding hot water burned my body so severely that it left me comatose for three days and hospitalized for months. After I was released, infection entered my body. The infection came because the cleaning process was so painful and traumatic that there were times it could not be done properly. I know this was not done on purpose. It was heavy on my mother to watch me go through that kind of pain, and the battle for my life was overwhelming for both of us. I was hospitalized again, and I almost died again.

That burn left scars and physical issues I would battle well into womanhood. I was too young to understand pain, trauma, survival, or purpose. I did not have the words to explain what had happened to me, but my body carried the evidence long before my mouth could tell the story.

While I was coming in and out of a coma during those first three days, my mother came under attack too. Because I was saying, "I'm sorry, Mom. I'm not going to do it anymore," the authorities believed my mother had done it to me. They thought she had burned me herself. They took my mother into custody, held and questioned her, while her baby was fighting for life.

But once I came out of the coma and they were able to really talk to me, the truth came forth. I had been playing with my brothers, and I accidentally fell into the water. What I said confirmed what my siblings had already told them, and my mother was released.

Looking back, I understand that I was not the only one under attack in that season. My mother was under attack too, because the enemy knew she would play an intricate part in me becoming who I am today. Her refusal, her strength, her prayers, her protection, and her decision to stand between me and what others said could not be done became part of my survival.

The burn itself was severe, but it was when infection took hold in my leg that the doctors wanted my mother to allow them to amputate. They feared the infection would make me septic. They feared it could shut down my organs. They feared it could eventually kill me.

But my mother said no. They told her my leg would never grow - but it did. They said I would never walk unassisted - but I did. When man said no, God said yes. When man said it could not be done, God stepped in and did what only He could do.

Looking back, I see more than an accident. I see a spiritual assault. I believe the enemy caught a glimpse of my future. The glimpse was him peeping into what God had placed on my life before I ever understood it. He got a sense of the anointing, the gifts, the power, the call, the mantle, and the apostolic assignment God had hidden in me before the blaze was fully recognized, acknowledged, accepted, or understood. He did not want me to come into the fullness of what God had for me.

That is why the scalding water matters. The enemy was not merely trying to drown me. He was trying to use heat against heat. He tried to use the heat of scalding water to kill the heat of my purpose. He tried to put me out and take me out before the fire God placed in me could ever rise.

In the natural, an ember is a small piece of fire that may not look like a flame yet, but it is still alive. It can glow quietly beneath ash, carry heat when the blaze is not visible, and catch again when breath and fuel touch it. An ember may look small, but it is evidence that fire is still present.

Spiritually, the Ember is the light of God placed inside the believer. It is the measure, the seed, the hidden witness, and the sign that Heaven deposited purpose before the world had language for it. The enemy may attack the body, the mind, the identity, and the confidence, but what he is really after is the Ember - the call of God burning in a life.

The scalding water marked my body, but it could not extinguish my purpose. It could mark my skin, but it could not drown my calling. It could send my body into shock, but it could not erase what God had written concerning me.

The attack did not stop with the burn. As I grew, the scars on my body became visible evidence of what I had survived. Yet because people did not understand my story, my body became a target for mockery. I was ridiculed. I was bullied. I was made to feel ashamed of the very thing God had allowed me to survive.

What touched my body as a burn later tried to touch my identity as rejection. It came after my self-esteem, my confidence, and even my faith in God. The enemy wanted my scars to make me question my worth, my beauty, my purpose, and my place in the world.

But the ridicule made me radical. What was meant to shame me only sharpened me. What was meant to make me hide only made me rise. Every laugh, every stare, and every cruel word became fuel for the fire God was building inside of me.

The marks were what they could see, but they could not measure what God was forming within me. The bullying did not bury me. The rejection did not erase me. The shame did not silence me. It became part of the catalyst behind the flame that still burns in me today.

I choose to be GODLY by surrender and MANIAC by fire - daily. GODLIAC, I AM SHE. But this was only the beginning of God's acts in my life.

Burned? Yes.

Broken? No.

Bitter? Never.

Chapter One

The Glimpse and the Spiritual Assault

The enemy caught a glimpse of what God had placed in me before I ever knew how to name it.

Scripture Anchor: "The thief cometh not, but for to steal, and to kill, and to destroy..." —John 10:10

Before my heart and soul were ever set ablaze for God, my flesh was burned by scalding hot water - the very thing known to put fire out. In the natural, it looked like a tragic childhood accident. In the spirit, I now understand there was an assault against what God had hidden in me.

The glimpse was the enemy peeping into my future. He did not know everything God would do, because he is not God. But he sensed enough to attack. He sensed anointing before I understood anointing. He sensed power before I had language for power. He sensed gifts before I could recognize them. He sensed a call, a mantle, and an apostolic assignment before I could acknowledge, accept, or walk in the fullness of what God had placed on my life.

That is why some warfare starts before understanding. The enemy does not wait until a person knows who they are to begin fighting them. He attacks what carries threat. He attacks what carries promise. He attacks what carries seed. He attacks what carries witness. He attacks the fire while it is still hidden because he does not want the blaze to ever be fully seen.

In the natural, an ember is not a full flame, but it is still fire. It can glow beneath ash. It can hold heat when no blaze is visible. It may look small, but if breath and fuel touch it, it can catch again. An ember is proof that fire is still alive, even when others only see what covers it.

Spiritually, the Ember is the light of God placed inside the believer. It is the measure of faith, the seed of purpose, the hidden witness, and the God-given call that the enemy cannot create and cannot own. That was what the enemy was after. He was not only after my flesh. He was after the Ember. He was after the witness before the witness could speak. He was after the assignment before it could mature.

That is why the scalding water carries more meaning than ordinary water. The enemy was not merely trying to drown me. He was trying to use heat against heat. He tried to use the heat of scalding water to kill the heat of my purpose. He tried to put me out and take me out before the fire God placed in me could rise.

But what God had hidden in me was buried deeper than my flesh. The enemy could touch my skin, but he could not reach the Ember God placed in my spirit. That Ember was not small to Heaven. It carried the call, the assignment, the mantle, the office of apostleship, and the believers I would one day be assigned to witness to, encourage, pray for, cover, speak to, and ignite.

The burn put my body into shock, but it could not erase what God had written. The scalding water marked my flesh, but it could not extinguish my purpose. It could not cancel what Heaven had already assigned to my life. What happened to me was painful, but it was not final.

Jeremiah 29:11 declares, "For I know the thoughts that I think toward you, saith the LORD, thoughts of peace, and not of evil, to give you an expected end." God had thoughts before the enemy had plans. God had purpose before pain. God had destiny before destruction. God had an expected end before the scalding water ever touched me.

The enemy thought he was putting something out, but God was preserving something deeper. The water touched my flesh, but God's fire marked my soul. I was scalded, but it did not smother my purpose. It did not minimize the damage I would one day do to the kingdom of darkness. It did not stop, delay, or alter the plans God had for me.

Burned? Yes.

Broken? No.

Bitter? Never.

BUT GOD!!! ACTS. #GODLIAC

Chapter Two

When Man Said No, God Said Yes

Scripture Anchor: "Behold, I am the LORD, the God of all flesh: is there anything too hard for me?" —Jeremiah 32:27

Man said amputate. Man said my leg would never grow. Man said I would never walk unassisted. But God acted, and what man called impossible became evidence of God's authority.

The enemy came after the Ember, but God was already protecting what belonged to Him. The scalding water had burned my flesh, but it had not reached my purpose. It had not reached my destiny. It had not reached what Heaven had already written concerning my life. After I survived the first battle, another battle rose through infection. When infection took hold in my leg, the doctors feared it could make me septic, shut down my organs, and eventually kill me. That is when they wanted my mother to allow them to amputate.

From what they could see, the damage was too great and the burn was too deep. In some places, my flesh had been scalded so badly that they did not believe my leg had a future. That was the report of man. But my mother refused to let them destroy what God still had purpose for. She may not have known every detail of my calling. She may not have known the full weight of the witness I would one day carry. She may not have known that GODLIAC would ever come out of my testimony. But somewhere in her faith, she knew that man's report was not greater than God's power.

My mother's faith was under pressure too. While I was coming in and out of a coma, her name was misunderstood, her heart was pierced by accusation, and her child was fighting for life. But God brought her through that accusation, and then He used her faith to stand between me and a report that wanted to remove what God still had purpose for. She said no when the doctors said amputate. She said no when fear said surrender. She said no when man's report looked final.

They said my leg would never grow, but it did. They said I would never walk unassisted, but I did. They said limitation, but God said movement. They said loss, but God said life. They said impossible, but God stepped into impossible and made my flesh testify. That was not luck. That was not chance. That was not my strength. I was a child lying in a body that could not fight for itself. If God had not stepped in, the story could have gone another way. But when God has purpose on a life, no diagnosis, no report, no limitation, and no attack can overrule His Word.

Jeremiah 32:27 still speaks over my life. Not the scald burn. Not the infection. Not the report. Not the leg they wanted to remove. Not the walk they said would never happen. Not the purpose the enemy tried to stop before it could stand. God did not need permission from the doctors to perform His Word. He did not need agreement from the report. He did not need the natural circumstances to look favorable. He is the God of all flesh, and when He decides that purpose shall live, even the flesh has to respond to His authority.

My leg became more than a leg. It became evidence. My walk became more than movement. It became witness. Every step I took became a quiet testimony that God had stepped into the matter and overruled what man said could not be done. The enemy wanted my flesh to become evidence against me, but God made my flesh evidence for His glory. The same leg they said would not grow became proof that God still performs miracles. The same walk they said would not happen became proof that when God says yes, no man's no can cancel it.

This was the next stage of the fire. The Ember had survived the assault, and now God began adding fuel. In the natural, fuel is the source that keeps a fire alive and gives it something to burn from. Spiritually, the report, the refusal, my mother's faith, and the miracle of my walk became fuel for the testimony. The enemy thought the doctor's report would weaken the fire, but God used it to feed the witness. Every "no" from man became more fuel for God's "yes." Every impossible word spoken over my flesh became another place for God to prove His authority. The same report that was meant to confirm defeat became the fuel God used to show that purpose was still alive.

I did not understand it then, but my flesh was already preaching. My leg was already preaching. My walk was already preaching. Before my mouth had words, my life was already saying that God acts. When man said no, God said yes. The report was real, but God had the final say.

Burned? Yes.

Broken? No.

Bitter? Never.

BUT GOD!!! ACTS. #GODLIAC

Chapter Three

The World Called Me Burnt, But My Mother Called Me Beautiful

The world called me burnt. My mother called me beautiful. But God called me His.

Scripture Anchor:
"Death and life are in the power of the tongue..." — Proverbs 18:21

The enemy could not kill the ember, and he could not stop God from turning my body into evidence, so he came after the next place he thought he could reach: my identity. If he could not erase the witness from my body, he would try to make me ashamed of the witness I carried. If he could not stop my leg from growing, he would try to make me hate the leg that survived. If he could not take my life, he would try to damage how I saw myself living it.

As I grew older, the scars on my body became visible evidence of what I had survived. But to children who did not understand my story, those scars became something to mock. I was from a small town called Hughes, Arkansas, a small town in the Delta where we did not have much, but we had each other. Still, children can be harsh. They can be critical. They can make jokes about what they do not understand, and because they did not understand my scars, they made my body a target.

From kindergarten through sixth grade, I cried a lot. Almost every day, some part of my day carried a reminder that people saw the scars before they saw me. It did not matter what I wore. If I wore pants, they knew. If I wore warm-ups or sweatsuits trying to cover my leg, they still knew. Somehow the wound I survived became the name they tried to give me.

They called me burnt this and burnt that. They called me burnt biscuit. Even when children played, the cruelty followed me. There were times they did not want me on their team, and the words came out sharp and simple: do not let the burnt girl play. Those words were not just playground words.

They were seeds. They were attempts to make the evidence of survival become a place of shame.

The burn marked my body, but the ridicule tried to mark my identity. The enemy wanted the mockery to become my name. He wanted rejection to sit where confidence belonged. He wanted shame to grow where purpose was planted. He wanted me to look at what God had preserved and see only damage.

But God had placed me inside the care of a mother who knew how to speak life.

When I came home crying, my mother did not let the world's words become the final words over me. She would tell me, "Chelle, you beautiful." She would tell me, "Chelle, don't worry about what they say." She would remind me, "Chelle, that don't define you. That don't make you. I didn't name you burnt biscuit."

Those words were more than comfort. They were covering. They were correction against the enemy's language. They were life spoken into the same places the world was trying to wound. My mother built me when the enemy was trying to tear me down. She built me when ridicule tried to weigh me down. She built me when my self-esteem was being stripped away by people too young to understand the damage their words could do.

This was the next stage of the fire. In the natural, kindling may look small, dry, and unnoticed, but it carries the potential to catch. Spiritually, my mother's words became kindling around the ember. Every affirmation, every correction, every reminder that I was beautiful and not defined by their words gave the fire something to hold on to. The enemy was trying to plant shame, but my mother was planting life.

Proverbs 18:21 says death and life are in the power of the tongue, and I lived the truth of that scripture as a child. The words spoken over me mattered. The cruel words tried to destroy, but my mother's words helped preserve. The mockery tried to name me, but her voice kept reminding me that I was not what they called me.

The world called me burnt, but my mother called me beautiful. And above every voice, God called me His.

The enemy wanted the scars to make me question my worth, my beauty, my purpose, and my place in the world. But what was meant to break me began to build something in me. The ridicule did not bury me. The rejection did not erase me. The shame did not silence me. It became part of the catalyst behind the flame that would one day burn in me for God.

I did not know it then, but kindling was being placed around the ember. My mother's words were feeding what God had preserved. The same mouth the enemy wanted to fill with shame would one day speak witness. The same child who came home crying would one day become a woman who could tell another child, "Baby, it is not worth destroying yourself. You are more than what they called you. You are more than what happened to you. God still has purpose for your life."

The ridicule was real, but it was not final. The names hurt, but they did not become my identity. The scars were visible, but they were not the deepest thing about me. God had already placed something greater inside of me, and through my mother's love, faith, and words, He kept protecting the fire.

Burned? Yes.

Broken? No.

Bitter? Never.

The world called me burnt, but my mother called me beautiful.

BUT GOD!!! ACTS.
#GODLIAC

Chapter Four

When Tears Turned Into Toughness

I stopped crying, but I had not yet healed. The tears became toughness, and the pain learned how to defend itself.

Scripture Anchor:
"And be not conformed to this world: but be ye transformed by the renewing of your mind..." — Romans 12:2

There comes a point when pain stops looking like tears and starts looking like toughness. For years, I cried because of what people said. I cried because of how they looked at me. I cried because the scars on my body made me a target for words I was too young to know how to carry. But as I got older, something shifted.

In Hughes, Arkansas, kindergarten through sixth grade were all in the same school. Going into seventh grade meant I would be moving over with the high school students, and my mother knew I could not carry myself into that next season the same way I had carried myself in the last one. That summer, she talked to me over and over again. She told me I could not go over there crying like I used to. She told me I had to love myself, embrace myself, believe in myself, and stop letting what people said discourage me.

She was not teaching me to become hard. She was teaching me to stand. She was teaching me that my leg did not define me, that my character mattered, that my attitude mattered, and that the way I carried myself would teach others how to treat me. Her words were meant to strengthen me, not harden me, but pain has a way of twisting even good instruction when healing has not had time to finish its work.

I did stop crying, but part of me also became harder. I developed an attitude that said words could not hurt me anymore, but underneath that attitude was still a wound that had not fully healed. If I caught someone looking at me the wrong way, I was ready to fight. I had learned how to stop the tears, but I had not yet learned how to surrender the pain.

That was where the enemy tried to get glory from what I had survived. He could not stop me from living, and he could not stop my mother from speaking life into me, so he tried to turn my survival into defense. He tried to make my protection become anger. He tried to make my strength become hardness. He tried to make me carry myself in a way that looked fearless on the outside but was still wounded underneath.

This was the smoldering stage of the fire. In the natural, smoldering is a slow burn. The flame may not be fully visible yet, but heat is present, and sometimes the first thing people notice is the scent. Spiritually, I was smoldering. Something was burning in me, but it had not yet become holy flame. Pain was present. Heat was present. A warning was present. The ember had survived, kindling had been placed around it, but now the slow burn of what I had lived through was beginning to show.

Smoldering can be dangerous because it looks controlled while something is still burning beneath the surface. That was me. I looked stronger, but strength without healing can become defense. I looked tougher, but toughness without surrender can become anger. I was no longer crying every day, but that did not mean every wound was healed.

Romans 12:2 speaks to this because transformation does not happen only on the outside. It happens through the renewing of the mind. God did not just want me to stop crying. He wanted to heal what made the tears necessary. He did not just want me to survive the ridicule. He wanted to transform the way I saw myself, the way I carried pain, and the way I responded to what had tried to break me.

Looking back, I can see that even then, God was working. He was showing me that survival is not the same as wholeness. He was showing me that strength without healing can still leave a person bound. He was showing me that the fire in me needed to become holy, not just hot.

The enemy wanted me to become bitter, angry, defensive, and destructive. But God was still protecting the purpose beneath the pain. Even in that season, the smoldering was not the end of the fire. It was another sign that something in me was still alive, still burning, and still waiting for God to breathe on it.

I stopped crying, but I still needed healing. I became tough, but God wanted me whole. The pain smoldered, but it did not consume my purpose.

Burned? Yes.

Broken? No.

Bitter? Never.

The tears turned into toughness, but God was still after my healing.

BUT GOD!!! ACTS.
#GODLIAC

Chapter Five

The Smoke Before the Flame

They could see the marks, but they could not measure the fire God was forming beneath them.

Scripture Anchor: "A bruised reed shall he not break, and the smoking flax shall he not quench..." — Isaiah 42:3

Before a flame is fully seen, smoke often rises first. In the natural, smoke is evidence that heat has touched something. It can move through a room before the fire is located. It can be seen by everyone present, and everything near it can come away carrying the smell. Smoke clings. It gets into fabric, hair, walls, and memory. Sometimes the hardest part is not seeing the smoke; it is getting the smell out after the smoke has touched everything around it.

Spiritually, smoke can work the same way. It can rise from pain, fear, rejection, anger, shame, and confusion. It can fill the atmosphere around a person until vision becomes cloudy and breath becomes hard. Smoke can make what is false feel real, and that is how fear begins to operate. Fear can become false evidence appearing real, a smoke screen that makes the believer respond to what is suggested instead of what God has spoken.

That is what the enemy wanted smoke to do in me. He wanted the smoke of shame to make me forget there was fire. He wanted the smoke of rejection to blind me from purpose. He wanted the smoke of pain to convince me that what God placed inside of me was destruction instead of formation. He wanted me to misuse the fire in me for rage, revenge, attitude, and fighting. He wanted the heat in me to burn the wrong way.

People could see my scars, but they could not see the heat beneath the surface. They could see the marks, but they could not measure what God was forming. They could see what happened to my body, but they could not understand what God was doing in my spirit.

The smoke also carried a scent. 2 Corinthians 2:14-16 speaks of the savour, or fragrance, of the knowledge of Christ being made manifest. The enemy recognizes scent. He knows when something belongs to God. He may not understand the whole assignment, but he can sense when purpose has been touched by Heaven. That is why the smoke mattered. It was evidence that something had been burning, even before the flame could be fully seen.

The tears were smoke. The toughness was smoke. The ache in me was smoke. The fight in me was smoke. The refusal to be buried by their words was smoke. It was not all holy yet, but it was evidence that something inside of me was alive, burning, and waiting for God to breathe on it.

The enemy wanted me trapped in the smoke. He wanted the smoke to suffocate the witness before the flame could rise. He wanted to put me out and take me out. But God was still working beneath the smoke, forming voice beneath hurt, strength beneath rejection, boldness beneath ridicule, and witness beneath the scars.

The smoke was not the end of the fire. It was the warning that the flame was coming. What the enemy meant to suffocate me only revealed that fire was still present.

Burned? Yes.

Broken? No.

Bitter? Never.

The smoke rose, but it could not hide the flame God was forming. And the enemy don't want that smoke.

BUT GOD!!! ACTS. #GODLIAC

Chapter Six

The Spark Became a Warning

The ridicule did not bury me. It struck something in me, and the spark became a warning.

Scripture Anchor: "For thou wilt light my candle: the LORD my God will enlighten my darkness." — Psalm 18:28

Smoke tells you fire is present, but a spark tells you fire is ready to show itself. In the natural, a spark may look small, but it is not harmless. It carries possibility. It carries warning. If the right breath reaches it and the right fuel is near it, what looked small can become flame.

Spiritually, the spark was my first visible sign that the calling was still alive. It was not just attitude. It was not just toughness. It was not just a child deciding not to cry anymore. Beneath all of that, God was protecting my purpose, my mantle, my voice, and the apostolic call that would one day help me stand, speak, write, witness, and carry the fire into places the enemy never wanted me to reach.

The ridicule did not stop. The scars did not disappear. The memories did not vanish. But something in me began to shift. I was no longer only the child who cried because of what they called me. Something inside me started rising against the words that were meant to bury me.

I did not understand it all then, and I did not always know how to carry it the right way, but a refusal began to form in me. I refused to let their names become my name. I refused to let their rejection become my identity. I refused to let their cruelty be the final voice over my life.

Psalm 18:28 says, "For thou wilt light my candle: the LORD my God will enlighten my darkness." That scripture speaks to what God does when darkness tries to surround purpose. He lights what the enemy tried to bury. He brings illumination where pain tried to create confusion. He causes something inside the believer to burn again when life tried to leave them dim.

The spark in me was not always pretty. Sometimes it looked like attitude. Sometimes it looked like toughness. Sometimes it looked like anger because I had not yet learned how to turn pain over to God. But underneath what looked rough on the outside, something deeper was happening. God was keeping the fire alive.

What was meant to shame me sharpened me. What was meant to make me hide made me rise. What was meant to silence me began forming a voice. The enemy thought ridicule would make me small, but God used it to awaken something in me that refused to disappear.

This was the spark stage. The Ember had survived. The fuel had been added. The kindling had been placed. The smoldering had started. The smoke had risen. Now the spark was showing. It was the warning that purpose was still alive, that the witness would speak one day, and that what the enemy tried to bury was beginning to rise.

I did not know GODLIAC was coming. I did not know the testimony would become a book. I did not know the fire would become a brand, a witness, and a declaration. But God knew. And because God knew, He kept lighting what the enemy kept trying to put out.

Burned? Yes.

Broken? No.

Bitter? Never.

The spark became a warning that the fire was still alive.

BUT GOD!!! ACTS. #GODLIAC

Chapter Seven

The Flame Became Visible

The pain did not disappear. It caught fire, and what was hidden in me began to show.

Scripture Anchor: "And we know that all things work together for good to them that love God..." — Romans 8:28

A spark is the warning, but a flame is the evidence that something has caught. In the natural, a flame can be seen. It gives off heat and light. It announces that what was once hidden has now become visible.

Spiritually, that is what began happening in me. The hurt and pain did not disappear, but they stopped sitting in me the same way. What once tried to crush me began turning into something God could use. The things that should have made me hide started pressing purpose to the surface. I did not know how to name it then, but something in me was changing.

Romans 8:28 does not mean everything that happens is good. It means God is powerful enough to work all things together for good for those who love Him and are called according to His purpose. God did not call the burn good. He did not call the ridicule good. He did not call the shame good. But He took what was painful, unfair, and meant for destruction, and He began working purpose through it.

This was the flame stage. The Ember had survived. The fuel had been added. The kindling had been placed. The smoldering had started. The smoke had risen. The spark had warned that calling was still alive. Now the flame was becoming visible.

It showed up in the way I began to carry myself. It showed up in the boldness forming beneath the wound. It showed up in the refusal to keep shrinking beneath what people said. It showed up in a witness that made me harder to silence, harder to bury, and harder to convince that my scars had the final say.

The flame was not all-consuming yet. It was not fully sanctified yet. It was not fully surrendered yet. Some of that heat still carried pain. Some of it still carried defense. Some of it still carried the need to prove I was more than what they called me. But even there, God was working. He was taking the heat of my life and turning it toward purpose.

The enemy wanted me bitter, but God was making me bold. The enemy wanted me ashamed, but God was making me aware that there was more to me than what happened. The enemy wanted me hidden, but God was bringing the flame forward.

I did not know GODLIAC was being formed. I did not know the Godly and the maniac in me would one day have a name. I did not know the fire I carried would become language, witness, apparel, and declaration. But I can look back now and see that the flame was already there.

It was not madness. It was not rebellion. It was not just attitude. It was a flame looking for surrender. It was purpose trying to rise out of pain. It was the beginning of a radical devotion that would one day refuse to be lukewarm, refuse to be silent, and refuse to water down what God had placed in my spirit.

Burned? Yes.

Broken? No.

Bitter? Never.

The hurt and pain kindled a flame, and the flame became visible.

BUT GOD!!! ACTS. #GODLIAC

Chapter Eight

Godly by Surrender, Maniac by Fire

I became Godly by surrender, but the fire made me radical.

Scripture Anchor: "Present your bodies a living sacrifice, holy, acceptable unto God..." — Romans 12:1

A flame can be seen, but ignition changes the atmosphere. In the natural, ignition is the moment a fire receives what it needs to burn with force. It is the place where what was hidden, smoking, sparking, and flaming begins to take over.

Spiritually, ignition is where the fire begins to agree with purpose. It is where the believer stops only surviving what happened and starts surrendering what remains. It is where pain no longer gets to lead the story. It is where witness begins to take shape. It is where the fire stops burning wild and starts burning holy.

That is what happened in me. The fire that began as survival could not stay survival. The flame that started beneath pain could not stay buried beneath my story. At some point, what God had preserved in me had to become surrendered to Him. It had to become holy. It had to become purpose. It had to become more than defense, more than toughness, and more than proof that I survived.

That is where GODLIAC was born. GODLIAC is not just a name. It is revelation. It is the place where Godly and maniac meet. Not maniac as madness, but maniac as radical devotion. It is the part of me that refuses to be lukewarm about a God who has never been casual with me.

For me, GODLIAC became language for a testimony that survived pain, pressure, ridicule, rejection, and shame, and then surrendered every surviving part back to God. It is not a fire finding its way back to Him as if He had lost it. It is God reclaiming, naming, and directing what He preserved all along.

Romans 12:1 speaks to surrender because the fire in me could not remain under the authority of pain. I had to present myself to God. I had to let Him govern the heat, the passion, the boldness, the voice, and the witness. What I survived could not lead me; God had to lead what survived.

I am not casual about what God has done for me because I know what He brought me through. I am not ashamed of my scars because they are no longer signs of defeat. They are evidence of a spiritual war and proof that God had the final say. The enemy thought he could use my body as evidence against me, but God turned my body into evidence for His glory.

Ignition is when the fire no longer belongs to pain, anger, shame, or defense. It belongs to God. The fire in me became more than something I carried. It became something I surrendered. And once I surrendered it, God gave it purpose, language, witness, and name.

GODLIAC. Godly by surrender. Maniac by fire.

Burned? Yes.

Broken? No.

Bitter? Never.

The flame found surrender, and ignition gave the fire a name.

BUT GOD!!! ACTS. #GODLIAC

Chapter Nine

All-Consuming Fire

The water marked my body, but God's fire marked my soul.

Scripture Anchor: "For our God is a consuming fire." — Hebrews 12:29

Ignition gives the fire a name, but all-consuming fire gives the fire authority. In the natural, consuming fire does not stop at the edges. It moves through what can burn until what cannot remain is gone. Spiritually, God's all-consuming fire does not come to destroy what belongs to Him. It comes to consume what cannot remain attached to His purpose.

This is the fire of God. It is not the scalding water that burned my body. It is not destructive fire. It is holy fire, refining fire, purifying fire. It burns away what tried to become part of the identity but was never part of the calling.

The enemy wanted water to put me out, but God used His refining fire to reveal me. He used it to expose what needed healing, purify what had been contaminated by shame, refine what had survived pressure, restore what had been damaged, reveal what He had been forming, and resurrect what the enemy thought was dead.

That is the work of the all-consuming fire. It does not leave the old nature comfortable. It does not let false identity stay in place. It does not let bitterness build a home in the heart. It does not allow shame to keep speaking louder than God. When God's fire begins to consume, it goes after everything that tries to sit in the seat of purpose.

It consumed the lie that I was what they called me. It consumed the shame that tried to make me hide. It consumed the fear that tried to make me shrink. It consumed the bitterness that could have grown from rejection. It consumed the anger that pain tried to justify. It consumed the need to be defined by what happened.

This was not God erasing my testimony. This was God purifying what my testimony would carry. The scar remained, but shame lost its authority. The memory remained, but bondage lost its hold. The story remained, but the wound no longer owned the ending.

Hebrews 12:29 declares that our God is a consuming fire, and I understand that differently now. His fire did not come to consume my who. My who belonged to Him. His fire came to consume what tried to cover my who. It came to burn through the false names, false labels, false identity, and pain that tried to become personality.

This is where the fire became holy, not because I had never hurt, not because I had never been angry, and not because I had always responded perfectly, but because God took the heat of pain and brought it under His authority. He took survival and turned it into surrender. He took what could have made me bitter and used it to make me burn for Him.

God's refining work had to reach my heart, my mind, my memory, my identity, and my surrender. Everything that could not go with purpose had to burn away. Everything that would have poisoned the witness had to be consumed. Everything that would have made me carry the testimony wrong had to lose its power.

And when God's fire touched those places, I could not go back the same. I could not see myself the same. I could not carry the scars the same. I could not let the enemy name me the same. I could not let the past rule me the same.

The water marked my body, but God's fire marked my soul. That mark became more than survival. It became identity. It became witness. It became GODLIAC. It became holy fire made visible.

Burned? Yes.

Broken? No.

Bitter? Never.

The fire consumed what could not remain, and revealed what God had preserved.

BUT GOD!!! ACTS. #GODLIAC

Chapter Ten

Godly Acts: Wear the Witness

My scars became proof that I survived. My leg became proof that God still performs miracles. My walk became proof that when God says yes, no diagnosis, no report, no limitation, and no attack can overrule His Word.

Scripture Anchor:
"Ye are our epistle written in our hearts, known and read of all men." — 2 Corinthians 3:2

When God acts and His refining work consumes what cannot remain, it leaves something behind. It leaves evidence. It leaves proof. It leaves a witness that says God was present, God moved, and God changed the ending.

That is what Godly Acts are.

They are the places where God steps into what man cannot fix, what the enemy cannot finish, and what the natural cannot explain. They are the moments when the I AM shows up Himself and leaves evidence that the situation did not end the way it could have ended because God acted.

For me, the witness was already in my body before my mouth ever knew how to tell the story. My scars were not just marks. My leg was not just a limb. My walk was not just movement. They were evidence. They were proof that God had stepped into the matter and overruled what could have destroyed me.

The enemy wanted my body to become evidence against me, but God made my body evidence for His glory. What was supposed to shame me became something God could use. What was supposed to silence me became something that now speaks. What was supposed to make me hide became part of the witness I now carry.

That is why witness cannot stay hidden forever.

A witness is not only something you say. A witness is something you become. When God brings you through fire, the proof of His hand begins to live in you. It shows in how you stand, how you speak, how you survive, how you forgive, how you heal, and how you refuse to let the enemy have the final word over your story.

2 Corinthians 3:2 says we are epistles, known and read of all men. That means a life can be read. A testimony can be seen. A witness can walk into a room before a person ever opens their mouth. People may not know every detail of what you survived, but they can still read the evidence of God's hand on your life.

That is the heart of GODLIAC. The Birth of GODLIAC Apparel

GODLIAC was birthed from the same place this testimony came from: fire, survival, obedience, and faith. It is more than a name on clothing. It is the outward witness of what God has done inwardly. The book tells the story, but the apparel carries the witness.

Every shirt, every phrase, and every declaration is designed to speak before a person ever opens their mouth. Some people may never ask what you have survived, but they may read what you are wearing. They may see a message on a shirt and be reminded that God still heals, still delivers, still covers, and still acts.

That is why GODLIAC is not just fashion. It is ministry in motion. It is testimony made visible. It is faith with fire on it. It is a way for believers to wear what they know: that the enemy did not get the final word, that shame does not own their story, and that God can turn what tried to destroy them into a witness others can see.

When I say, "God Acted. Wear the Witness," I am not just talking about apparel. I am talking about wearing the evidence of God's hand with boldness, humility, and purpose.

GODLIAC is not just apparel. It is wearable witness. It is testimony carried. It is evidence made visible. It is a declaration that says God brought me through something, and I refuse to hide the proof of His hand.

The world may see a shirt, but God sees a witness. The world may see words, but Heaven knows the fire behind them. The world may call it fashion, but for the one wearing it, it may be language for survival, healing, identity, restoration, and purpose.

This is what the fire left behind.

The ember survived. The fuel was added. The kindling caught. The smoldering warned. The smoke rose. The spark appeared. The flame became visible. Ignition gave the fire a name. The all-consuming fire burned away what could not remain. Now the witness had to be worn.

Not just worn on fabric, but worn in the life.

Worn in the walk.

Worn in the voice.

Worn in the faith.

Worn in the refusal to be ashamed.

To wear the witness is to stop letting the enemy clothe your identity in shame. It means carrying the proof of God's hand with humility and boldness, not for attention, but because another survivor may need to see that pain did not get the final word.

Somebody needs to see that scars can still carry glory. Somebody needs to know that what happened does not have to become who they are. Somebody needs to read a witness before they have strength to tell their own story.

That is why GODLIAC speaks to the season someone is standing in. Not everyone has my burn testimony, but everybody has something. Everybody has a fire, a report, a scar, a season, a battle, a place where God had to act. GODLIAC gives language to the witness. It gives the believer a way to declare that what touched them did not define them, what fought them did not finish them, and what they survived can become testimony.

Revelation 12:11 declares:

"And they overcame him by the blood of the Lamb, and by the word of their testimony..."

The blood is the victory. The testimony is the evidence that the victory reached your life. That is why the enemy fights witness so hard. He does not want people to speak what God brought them through. He does not want pain turned into purpose, scars turned into evidence, or testimony turned into ministry.

But God's acts leave proof.

And when God leaves proof, the witness must speak.

My scars speak.

My leg speaks.

My walk speaks.

My survival speaks.

My healing speaks.

My fire speaks.

GODLIAC speaks.

Burned? Yes.

Broken? No.

Bitter? Never.

God acted, and the witness remains.

BUT GOD!!! ACTS.
#GODLIAC

Chapter Eleven

Go Ye Therefore: The Fire Has to Spread

Before GODLIAC became a brand, it was a testimony. Before it became apparel, it was survival. Before it became a message, it was evidence.

Scripture Anchor:
"Go ye therefore, and teach all nations..." — Matthew 28:19

Fire was never meant to stay hidden in one place. Once fire catches, it moves. It reaches. It spreads. What begins as an ember can become a flame, and what becomes a flame can become a blaze. But when God's all-consuming fire has done its work in a life, it does not stop with the person who survived it. It becomes witness. It becomes assignment. It becomes something that must go.

That is why GODLIAC could not stay inside of me. The testimony was too heavy to hide. The witness was too alive to bury. The fire had burned through too much for me to act like God had done nothing. When God acts, the witness remains, and when the witness remains, it must speak.

Matthew 28:19 says, "Go ye therefore, and teach all nations." That command is not only about distance. It is about movement. It is about carrying what God placed in you beyond the place where it happened. It is about taking the fire, the testimony, the Word, the healing, the revelation, and the witness into the earth so somebody else can see that God still acts.

Coming through the process does not make us silent people. It makes us sent people. God does not bring us through just so we can say we survived. He brings us through so our survival gives Him glory. He brings us through so another person can look at what should have destroyed us and see evidence that God is real, God is present, and God still has power to change an ending.

The witness in me had to become more than memory. It had to become mission. It had to become language for somebody else who did not yet know how to name what they were carrying. It had to become a witness for the one who had been burned by life, marked by pain, mocked by people, and still did not know that the very thing they were ashamed of could become evidence in the hands of God.

That is where GODLIAC carries weight. GODLIAC is not just something to wear. It is something that speaks. It speaks to the believer who has survived fire, warfare, rejection, trauma, shame, pain, and pressure, but still stands as evidence that God had the final say. It speaks to the person who does not look like what they have been through because God's fire burned away what should have taken them down and revealed what would carry them forward.

The world may call it apparel, but I know it as witness in motion. I know it as testimony carried. I know it as holy fire made visible. I know it as the language God gave me so what He did in me could do something through me.

The fire has to spread because people are still sitting in smoke. People are still wearing shame. People are still listening to names God never called them. People are still looking at scars and thinking the scar is the end of the story. Somebody needs to see a witness before they can speak their own. Somebody needs to read evidence before they believe God can touch their situation too.

That is why the fire cannot stay contained.

A contained fire may warm one room, but a sent fire can light another life. A hidden testimony may comfort the one who carries it, but a released testimony can help someone else survive. When God brings us through, the glory belongs to Him, and the witness belongs in the earth.

This is the next stage of the fire. The ember survived. The fuel was added. The kindling caught. The smoldering warned. The smoke rose. The spark appeared. The flame became visible. Ignition gave the fire a name. The all-consuming fire consumed what could not remain. God acted, and the witness remained. Now the fire had to go.

It had to go beyond my body, beyond my scars, beyond my childhood, beyond my pain, beyond my own testimony. It had to go into a brand, into a book, into a declaration, into apparel, into ministry, into every place God assigned my witness to reach.

The enemy wanted me dead before the witness could speak, but God preserved me so the witness could go.

The fire refined me.

The fire revealed me.

The fire resurrected purpose in me.

Now the fire has to spread.

Burned? Yes.

Broken? No.

Bitter? Never.

God acted, the witness remained, and the fire had to go.

BUT GOD!!! ACTS.
#GODLIAC

Chapter Twelve

Full Circle: Nothing Lost in God

The first sermon I ever preached was "Catch on Fire, Lest You Be Set on Fire: The All-Consuming Fire of God."

Scripture Anchor:
"Gather up the fragments that remain, that nothing be lost." —John 6:12

God brought something back to me full circle. The first sermon I ever preached was called, "Catch on Fire, Lest You Be Set on Fire: The All-Consuming Fire of God." At the time, I preached what God gave me, but now I can see my whole life inside that message. I can see the burn. I can see the scars. I can see the ridicule. I can see the tears. I can see the fire that was working in me before I had language for it.

That sermon was not random. It was proof that God's hand had been on me from childhood until now. It was proof that the fire had always been part of the message. It was proof that what I lived, what I survived, what I preached, and what God birthed through me were all connected.

The revelation of that sermon was this: either we catch on fire for God while we are living, while we have breath in our bodies, while we still have time to show forth His glory, or we face fire apart from Him. One way or another, fire is appointed. The question is whether we will surrender to the holy fire that refines, restores, reveals, and resurrects, or reject God and face the fire that was never meant for His children.

That is not a light revelation. That is not a soft message. That is the weight of God's holiness. We cannot water Him down. We cannot shrink His authority. We cannot reduce His fire to something comfortable. God is loving, but He is holy. God is merciful, but He is righteous. God is gracious, but He is still a consuming fire.

When I look back now, I understand something I did not fully understand then. The enemy can do what he can, but he can never do what he wants. He can only go as far as God allows. He could touch my body, but he could not destroy my purpose. He could mark my skin, but he could not erase my witness. He could send smoke, but he could not stop the fire. He could bring pain, but he could not overrule the plan.

That is why John 6:12 speaks so deeply to this place in my testimony. After Jesus fed the multitude, He told His disciples to gather up the fragments that remained, that nothing be lost. That is the God I know. He gathers fragments. He gathers broken places. He gathers rejected pieces. He gathers what people overlook, what pain scattered, what the enemy thought would never be useful again.

There is nothing missing, broken, or lacking in God. What looks like fragments to man can still become provision in the hands of God. What looks discarded to the world can still carry purpose in the Kingdom. What looked like pain in one season can become witness in another. God does not waste what is surrendered to Him.

The burn was not wasted. The tears were not wasted. The scars were not wasted. The ridicule was not wasted. The years of not understanding were not wasted. The sermon was not wasted. God gathered the fragments of my life and showed me that nothing was lost in Him.

Isaiah 46:10 says God declares the end from the beginning. That means God saw the whole circle before I ever walked through one part of it. He saw the child. He saw the burn. He saw the hospital room. He saw my mother's faith. He saw the scars. He saw the ridicule. He saw the sermon. He saw GODLIAC. He saw the book. He saw the witness. He saw the fire before I ever knew how to name it.

That is why I can say this with confidence: everything the enemy thought he was using to put me out became proof that God was preparing me to burn for Him.

The fire that touched me as a child did not end my story. It became part of the message God would later put in my mouth. The same all-consuming fire I preached about was the fire God had been revealing through my life all along. My life had been preaching before I ever stood to preach.

God's hand was on me then, and God's hand is on me now. He was not absent in the burn. He was not absent in the healing. He was not absent in the ridicule. He was not absent in the fire. He was gathering fragments the whole time.

This chapter brings the circle back around. The ember became fire. The fire became witness. The witness became language. The language became GODLIAC. And the message I preached at the beginning of my ministry was the same fire God had been writing through my life from the beginning.

Catch on fire for God now. Let His fire refine you now. Let His fire reveal you now. Let His fire restore you now. Let His fire use your witness now.

Because fire is appointed.

But in Christ, fire does not have to destroy you.

It can refine you.

It can reveal you.

It can resurrect what the enemy thought was dead.

Burned? Yes.

Broken? No.

Bitter? Never.

God gathered the fragments, and nothing was lost.

BUT GOD!!! ACTS.
#GODLIAC

Closing Chapter

Burned Yes, Broken No, Bitter Never

Whatever touched you did not define you. Whatever fought you did not finish you. Whatever season you survived can become a witness.

Scripture Anchor:
"We are troubled on every side, yet not distressed; we are perplexed, but not in despair; persecuted, but not forsaken; cast down, but not destroyed." — 2 Corinthians 4:8–9

This book began with my testimony, but it does not end with me. It began with the burn, the scars, the ridicule, the shame, the smoke, the fire, and the witness. But the purpose of the witness was never to make the reader only look at my story. It was to make the reader look at their own.

Everybody has something. Everybody has a fire. Everybody has a season. Everybody has a place where the enemy tried to mark them, name them, shame them, bury them, break them, or make them bitter. Everybody has something they had to survive, and if you keep living, life will bring you to a place where you will have to decide what voice gets the final word over your life.

Will it be what happened, or will it be what God said? Will it be the wound, or will it be the witness? Will it be the fire, or will it be what God brings out of the fire?

That is why this book is called Burned Yes, Broken No, Bitter Never.

Burned speaks to what happened. Broken speaks to what it was supposed to produce, but did not. Bitter speaks to what pain tried to leave behind, but could not. The reason brokenness did not win and bitterness did not take root is because God acted.

God acted when my body was burned. God acted when death tried to come back through infection. God acted when man said amputate. God acted when they said my leg would not grow. God acted when they said I would not walk unassisted. God acted when the world called me burnt, and my mother called me beautiful. God acted when the smoke rose, when the spark appeared, when the flame became visible, when ignition gave the fire a name, and when His all-consuming fire began to consume what could not remain.

The act was God moving. The witness is what remains.

That is why GODLIAC exists. GODLIAC speaks to the season someone is standing in. It speaks to the fire they are walking through. It speaks to the witness God is bringing out of it. Not everybody has my burn testimony, but everybody has a testimony. Everybody has a place where they need God to act. Everybody has a place where they need the natural to meet the supernatural. Everybody has a place where they need to know that what happened does not have to be the final word.

2 Corinthians 4:8–9 gives language to what it means to survive without being destroyed. Troubled, but not distressed. Perplexed, but not in despair. Persecuted, but not forsaken. Cast down, but not destroyed. That is the pattern. Touched, but not taken out. Pressed, but not crushed. Burned, but not broken. Tested, but not bitter.

This is not denial. This is witness. The pain was real. The fire was real. The scars were real. The attack was real. But God was real too, and His power was greater than what came against me.

So I leave this witness with you: what touched you did not define you. What fought you did not finish you. What burned you did not break you. What tested you does not have to make you bitter. What you survived can become witness, and what God brings out of the fire can be greater than the fire itself.

You may have been sick, but defeated does not have to be your name. You may have been rejected, but forgotten does not have to be your portion. You may have been wounded, but destroyed does not have to be your ending. You may have been pressed, delayed, attacked, overlooked, or scarred, but when God acts, the ending changes.

That is the pull of GODLIAC. It speaks to your season. It gives language to what God brought you through. It lets the believer declare that the enemy tried it, but God had the final say.

This was my testimony. Now look for your witness.

God acted.

The witness remains.

Wear the proof.

Burned? Yes.

Broken? No.

Bitter? Never.

BUT GOD!!! ACTS.
#GODLIAC

P.S. Hot Off the Press: Thus Says Abba

This is not an afterthought. This is the seal after the witness. After the testimony has spoken, after the chapters have walked through the burn, the scars, the ridicule, the smoke, the spark, the flame, the all-consuming fire, and the witness, Abba still speaks.

Abba says: I saw you before the fire touched you. I knew you before pain named you. I called you before the world could misunderstand you. I preserved what the enemy tried to destroy, and I gathered what life tried to scatter. Nothing surrendered to Me was lost.

The scar did not surprise Me. The smoke did not hide you from Me. The fire did not frighten Me. The report did not overrule Me. The words spoken against you did not rename you. The place where the enemy thought he was finishing you became the place where I began revealing the witness I had hidden in you.

You were never only what happened. You were never only what hurt. You were never only what people saw. You were never only the burn, the scar, the wound, the shame, the rejection, or the season you had to survive. You were Mine before the mark, Mine in the middle of the fire, and Mine after the smoke cleared.

This is why the witness must live. This is why the fire must spread. This is why the proof must be worn, spoken, written, carried, and released. Not so pain can be glorified, but so God can be glorified through what pain could not destroy.

To the one reading this: what touched you does not get to define you. What fought you does not get to finish you. What burned you does not get to break you. What tested you does not have to make you bitter. When you surrender the fragments to God, He knows how to gather them until nothing is lost.

So stand in the witness. Wear the proof. Speak what God brought you through. Let the fire do its holy work. Let the smoke clear. Let the ember breathe. Let the flame rise. Let the all-consuming fire of God reveal the who He hid with Christ in Him.

Burned? Yes. Broken? No. Bitter? Never.

Because Abba acted, the witness remains.

BUT GOD!!! ACTS.
#GODLIAC

Made in the USA
Coppell, TX
09 July 2026

83869428R00026